Your Environ

GENETICALLY Modified Food

Jen Green

Franklin Watts
London • Sydney

How to use this book

This series has been developed for group use in the classroom, as well as for students reading on their own. Its differentiated text allows students of mixed reading abilities to enjoy reading and talking about the same topic.

① The main text and ② picture captions give essential information in short, simple sentences. They are set in the © Sassoon font as recommended by the National Literacy Strategy document *Writing in the Early Years.* This font style helps students bridge the gap between their reading and writing skills.

③ Below each picture caption is a subtext that explains the pictures in greater detail, using more complicated sentence structures and vocabulary.

④ Text backgrounds are cream or a soft yellow to reduce the text/background contrast to support students with visual processing difficulties or other special needs.

GM crops

The main GM crops are ① soya, maize and rapeseed.

They can survive weedkiller or attack by insects.

⬆ **A field of rapeseed.** ②

③ Rapeseed is a crop used in cooking oils. GM scientists can now add a gene to rapeseed plants, so they can survive the general weedkiller. ④

PAPERBACK EDITION PRINTED 2007

© Aladdin Books Ltd 2004

Designed and produced by
Aladdin Books Ltd
2/3 Fitzroy Mews
London W1T 6DF

First published in 2004
in Great Britain by
Franklin Watts
338 Euston Road
London NW1 3BH

Franklin Watts Australia
Hachette Children's Books
Level 17/207 Kent Street
Sydney NSW 2000

A catalogue record for this book is available from the British Library.
Dewey Classification: 363.19' 2
ISBN 978-0-7496-7529-5

Printed in Malaysia

All rights reserved

Editor: Jim Pipe

Educational Consultant:
Jackie Holderness

Science Consultant:
Dr Sue Mayer, GeneWatch UK

Design:
Flick, Book Design and Graphics

Picture Research:
Brian Hunter Smart

CONTENTS

Introduction

GM is a new kind of science that is in the news at the moment.

Scientists are trying to produce better crops using a science called Genetic Modification, or GM.

GM works by changing genes, tiny parts inside plants and animals.

This book explains how GM works and what it can be used for.

⬆ **GM plants do not look different.**

From the outside, GM plants, such as tomatoes and wheat, don't look any different and they may not taste any different. For example, tomatoes with an extra gene taken from a fish will not tasty "fishy".

GM foods are in the news. People do not agree how safe they are.

GM foods are causing a big row at the moment. Some people feel that GM foods are an important invention. They believe that GM will help farmers to produce more food.

Other people worry that this new science will bring dangers. Some of them go on protest marches or destroy fields of GM crops. They do not want GM crops to affect other crops and animals nearby. That is why you hear a lot about GM in the news.

SAY NO TO GM!

What are GM foods?

Inside every plant and animal are groups of chemicals called genes. Genes control how living things work and grow.

Scientists can change plants and animals by changing their genes. We call this Genetic Modification, or GM, which means "changing the genes" of something.

GM food is any food that contains parts of GM plants or animals.

▷ **Genes make animals look like their parents.**

This zebra foal has stripes like its mother because she has passed on this particular feature to her baby through her genes.

Genes carry instructions for features such as shape, size and colour. They allow parents to pass on their features to their young. Genes work like plans for new living things, telling them how to grow and develop.

⬈ These melons are a GM crop.

Scientists can change the genes of plants in many different ways. Here, the genes of the melon were changed so that the melons ripen more slowly. This means they stay fresh for longer. Other GM crops have been changed so they can fight off insects or disease.

⬇ GM science can make tomatoes more juicy.

Farmers have always tried to produce the best possible crops. GM is the latest step in this effort to grow more food.

GM is one of a range of new sciences called biotechnology. This new branch of science may allow scientists to put living things to new uses, such as removing harmful waste and producing new medicines.

⬈ Many foods contain parts of GM crops.

TOMATO PUREE

Made with GM Tomatoes

400g

In some countries, you can buy GM crops like tomatoes. But foods such as soups, sauces and pastries may also contain GM ingredients, such as GM soya beans. Some labels tell you if a product contains GM ingredients, but not all.

7

How plants and animals grow

Plants, animals and people are made up of tiny units called cells.

Inside every cell are tens of thousands of different genes. Genes are made of a chemical called DNA. They control how cells grow.

When plants and animals reproduce, they pass on their genes to their young. That is why the young look and behave like their parents.

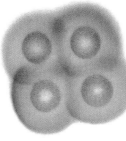

▷ Cells make up living things. There are billions of cells in your body.

Cells are the basic units of which living things are made. They are so tiny that they can only be seen using a powerful microscope. Simple living things, such as bacteria, are made up of just one cell.

More complicated plants and animals, including humans, have billions of cells. Most cells contain a nucleus, which acts as the control centre for the cell.

Genes guide this growing seedling.

A young oak tree sprouts from an acorn. Its cells contain genes with all the information it needs to grow into a tall tree. Its genes guide features such as the shape of its leaves, so it grows into an oak tree, not another type of tree. Thanks to its genes, one day the grown-up oak tree will produce its own acorns.

Inside your cells are genes. They make your hair fair or dark!

Inside the nucleus of every cell in your body are your genes. These are made up of DNA. DNA is a mix of four chemicals arranged in different ways. How these four chemicals are arranged spells out a code that controls how all the different parts of your body grow. This code allows genes to carry instructions for a particular feature, such as the colour of your hair or eyes.

Genes make you look like your mum and dad.

It is your genes which allow you to inherit features, such as the shape of your nose, from your parents. Before you were born, genes from your mum and dad combined in a unique way to make the tiny cell that grew into you. You inherited features from both your parents.

The parents' genes combine in a different way every time, which is why brothers and sisters look similar, but not exactly the same.

Changing plants and animals

Farmers have been changing crops and farm animals for thousands of years.

Farmers pick seeds from the best crops to grow more food. They breed their best animals. Over a long time, their herds grow bigger or make more milk.

GM is a new way of changing crops. It may help farmers to grow even more.

⬆ **Modern maize has large, juicy seeds.**

⬆ **Today's wheat has big grains.**

For thousands of years, farmers have been growing wheat for its tasty grains, which are ground into flour to make bread. The first wild wheat plants produced only small grains. Centuries ago, farmers began to improve the crop by saving seeds from the best plants to sow the following year.

You may have eaten maize or "sweetcorn". The first maize plants grew wild in Mexico and produced small seeds. Over many years, farmers improved the crop by selecting the best seeds to grow new plants from. We call this selective breeding.

Plants need plenty of water and nourishing minerals to grow well. Even prize crops won't grow well in dry or poor soil. Animals also need enough food and water to grow strong and healthy.

The environment can change plants and animals as well as genes. For example, some plants change over hundreds or thousands of years so that they can grow in drier areas. We say that they evolve.

◁ **Farmers try to breed large, healthy animals, like this cow.**

Over the years, farmers can also change animals, such as pigs and cattle, through breeding. They choose the cows that give the most milk or meat, to breed with their prize bulls. The young calves that inherit the best features from their parents are used to breed the next generation. So the farmer's herd gradually improves.

11

Modern farming

Farmers now produce more food than ever before. Tractors and other machines help them to work quickly.

Some modern farmers add chemicals to the soil to nourish crops. They also use poisons to kill pests such as insects.

Over the years, farmers have also bred many new plants and animals.

⇧ **These sheep produce lots of wool.**

⇧ **Farmers produce new types of apples.**

Farmers and gardeners have learned to produce new varieties of crops by crossing similar types of plants.

The resulting plant, called a hybrid, may combine the best qualities of both parent plants. For example, farmers can cross a juicy apple with another type of apple that can fight disease.

Farmers also develop new types of sheep by cross-breeding. For example, hill sheep farmers may cross tough local sheep, that can stand the cold, with a thick-fleeced breed from another area to produce a new hardy breed with thicker wool.

However, cross-breeding animals is slow. It can take many years.

Many farmers spray their crops to kill insects.

Many modern farmers spray poisons called herbicides on their fields to kill weeds. This is because the weeds take goodness from the soil that is needed for crops. Many farmers also spray their crops with poisons called pesticides. These poisons kill pests, such as insects, that eat their crops.

A brush is used to breed new sunflowers.

Most plants can only make seeds after they have been fertilised by dusty pollen from another plant. We call this pollination.

In nature, insects such as bees carry pollen from one plant to another. Gardeners can also transfer pollen from the flowers of one plant to another, using a paintbrush. By selecting the right plants, they can produce hybrid plants, such as sunflowers.

brush _____

pollen _____

flower _____

Why is GM different?

Farmers can change plants and animals by breeding. Breeding involves thousands of genes, so it can take a long time to work.

Scientists can now pick out genes that do a certain job. They add new genes to living things to change them in particular ways.

GM can be fast compared to breeding methods. But, like all new science, GM needs lots of testing.

◁ **Farmers took many years to breed large, juicy tomatoes.**

△ **GM changed these tomatoes very quickly.**

Tomatoes originally came from North and South America. The first wild tomato plants produced small, sweet fruits the size of grapes. Over many years, cross-breeding produced the large, juicy tomatoes we eat today.

Tomatoes go soft soon after they are picked because a gene in the plant triggers a special chemical. Scientists can change the plant's genes to stop this chemical being made. This makes the tomato ripen slowly, so it stays fresh for longer. Without GM, this change would have taken years of breeding.

GM can stop bugs from eating crops.

In North America, a caterpillar called the corn rootworm eats maize plants. They can destroy entire harvests. Scientists discovered that tiny bacteria in the soil make a poison called Bt that kills the young insects, but does not harm people.

GM scientists have now added the Bt poison gene to maize, to produce a crop which makes its own pest-killer. Traditional breeding methods could never have produced this result.

GM scientists may use animal genes to help plants survive frosts.

GM can also produce changes in living things that could never happen in nature. Fish that swim in icy polar seas have a chemical in their blood which stops them from freezing. Scientists could add the gene from the fish to plants. This might help the plants to survive cold, frosty weather.

How does GM work?

GM scientists take a gene from one living thing and put it into another. The new gene may change just one or two things in a plant or animal.

Scientists can also use GM to "switch off" a gene that causes an effect they do not want.

Scientists make these changes by changing tiny bacteria. They introduce the bacteria to plants or animals to change how they work.

▷ **Look at these bacteria. They are tiny living things.**

Bacteria are simple living things that are found everywhere, even inside plants, animals and people. Bacteria are so small they can only be seen through a microscope.

Some types of bacteria can cause illness, but most types are harmless. Using GM, scientists can change bacteria so that they can infect other plants with the changed genes.

GM scientists first add new genes to the tiny bacteria.

Bacteria contain tiny rings of DNA. These rings allow genes to move between different types of living things.

① GM scientists cut the rings open using special chemicals as "scissors".

② They add a new section of DNA, close the ring and then return it to the bacteria.

③ The bacteria now contain an altered gene.

The changed bacteria are mixed with plant cells in dishes.

Scientists add the bacteria to cells from the plant they want to change. They use dishes that contain a jelly with nutrients that will help the plant cells grow. The bacteria infect the plant cells, and some cells take up the altered gene.

Young plants grow from the cells.

When young plants grow from the altered cells, they are rooted in rich soil in greenhouses. As the young plants grow, scientists test them to see if the modification (change) has worked.

GM can make strawberries sweeter!

An example of GM is a new type of strawberry plant that produces sweeter strawberries. They do this by adding a gene that makes the plant produce more sugar.

Scientists add the "sweet" gene to bacteria. The bacteria are then mixed with cells from the strawberry plant in a dish. The changed strawberry cells are then encouraged to grow in strawberry plants. When these plants bear fruit, they are tested.

What are GM crops?

Maize

Soya beans

Rapeseed

GM science is about 30 years old. Scientists are still working out new ways to use GM. Meanwhile some U.S. farmers are planting GM crops.

The four main GM crops are soya, maize, cotton and rapeseed. Some of them can survive weedkiller. Other GM crops can survive attack by insects.

GM scientists are also working on crops that may taste better or grow faster.

▷ **Some GM plants can survive strong weedkiller.**

Rapeseed is a crop used in cooking oils. GM scientists can now add a gene to rapeseed plants, so they can survive the general weedkiller.

This means that the farmer can spray the plants just once, instead of several times. The farmer will save money on weedkiller, and fewer chemicals are used overall, which is kinder to nature.

GM cotton also contains a gene that kills insects.

In the past, cotton farmers had to spray their crops to protect them from insects. The Bt gene that protects maize from insects can also be added to cotton.

GM cotton crops with the added gene now kill the pests themselves, so farmers who grow these GM crops also use fewer chemicals.

Who makes GM crops?

The seeds that grow into GM plants are being made by just a few big companies in the United States and Europe.

The company that makes GM soya bean seeds also makes the weedkiller that can be used on the crop. So it sells the seeds and weedkiller to farmers as a package.

GM in the future

Some scientists believe that GM crops could one day put an end to hunger, one of the world's biggest problems.

They are trying to create crops that could grow in areas that are too dry or cold for farming today. But it may take a long time to create these crops.

⌂ **Scientists could use genes from this grass to create tough GM corn.**

GM scientists are working on GM corn that can grow in dry or cold areas. This could help to feed the world's poor. But people often starve because they have no money to buy food that they cannot grow themselves. So the new GM crops need to be cheap enough for farmers everywhere to buy.

◁ This soil is too dry and stony for crops to grow well.

Each year, many people from poor areas die of hunger, or from illnesses caused by not eating a healthy diet.

The soil in these regions may be too poor or salty for farming, or there may not be enough rain to water the crops.

◁ GM foods, such as rice, might be more healthy.

In poor parts of the world, some people get ill because they don't get enough vitamins in their food. In Asia, where the main food is rice, a lack of vitamin A can make people go blind.

Scientists have added a gene to rice that produces vitamin A. One day, GM rice could provide a vitamin-rich food.

▽ Scientists are creating GM pigs and fish.

Scientists are using GM to make animals grow bigger and faster. Growth genes are being added to salmon, pigs and sheep. Other genes are added to make animals with less fat and more meat.

However, changing genes in animals is much harder than in plants. Very few GM animals are healthy. Many of the pigs and sheep changed with human genes had serious illnesses.

Nature at risk

Many people think that GM foods are being grown without enough testing. They worry that genes from GM crops could escape and harm nature.

Some scientists also believe that GM crops could wipe out wild plants or create super-strong weeds.

Many people feel that GM crops should not be planted until we are absolutely sure they are safe.

▷ GM maize can kill harmless caterpillars.

Some people fear that GM crops containing pest-killing genes could damage insects that are not pests. Monarch butterfly caterpillars do not eat crops. However, tests have shown that some GM maize pollen can kill them. The same crops leak poison into the soil, where it could harm other living things.

GM crops could harm birds. ◁

Poison sprayed on fields or added to crops enters the food chain. When insects eat the crop, they absorb the poison. When they are in turn eaten by larger animals, the poison passes on. This means that birds and other animals could also be poisoned by GM crops.

GM could create "superweeds".

Over time, species of weeds change naturally, to suit their environment. They also change to cope with poisonous chemicals, so that the poisons no longer kill them.

Some people fear that if the gene that allows GM crops to cope with weedkiller got into a weed, it could change the weed too. This could create a "superweed" that farmers could no longer kill with poison. This picture shows how tough weeds can choke corn plants.

Bees could spread GM genes.

When plants flower, pollen is carried away on the wind, or by insects to fertilise other plants. Some people fear that pollen from GM crops could escape to fertilise ordinary crops. They worry that GM genes could spread through nature, out of scientists' control.

Health worries

There are different views about GM foods and our health.

When GM scientists create a new crop, they run tests to find out if the food is safe. Some scientists think that better tests are needed.

If GM crops do make people ill, we may not know the reason for many years. It is safer to carry out tests over a long time.

▷ GM soya beans could make some people ill.

Foods such as nuts are good for us, but they can cause bad reactions, called allergies. When some people eat these foods, they become ill.

In the 1990s, GM scientists added a brazil nut gene to soya plants, to make the crop more nourishing. However, tests showed that people who were allergic to nuts could react badly to the soya. So the experiment was stopped.

⬇ GM foods are tested on animals such as catfish.

One of the ways to test GM foods is to feed them to rats, fish or chickens. If the animals react badly, it is quite likely that people will, too. In one test, GM potatoes harmed the insides of rats that fed on them. In another test, pigs with an added gene to make them grow faster developed bone problems.

⬇ GM potatoes could be better for you.

GM scientists are experimenting with GM foods that may be better for us than ordinary foods. For example, GM science could create a potato that contains less starch. This potato would absorb less fat when fried, making it healthier.

But some scientists are worried about these "healthy" products. They think it is safer just to eat healthy food – and less chips!

In the supermarket

GM foods are now on sale in shops. In the United States, you can buy GM crops, such as tomatoes.

In Europe, foods such as soups, pastries and sauces may contain GM ingredients.

GM foods need clear labels, so people can choose whether or not to buy them.

▽ Can you buy GM fruit?

In the United States, you may see slow-ripening tomatoes and other GM crops in supermarkets. Most European supermarkets do not sell GM fruits or vegetables. But they may sell meat from animals that have been fed on GM foods.

Pasta

Crisps

△ Crisps and pizzas may contain GM rapeseed or soya.

Over half of all foods sold in U.S. supermarkets contain some GM. GM soya is used to make bread, biscuits, pizza and pasta. Cooking oil, crisps and margarine may contain GM rapeseed. But in Europe, many supermarkets have stopped using GM crops in food.

Pastry

Cheese

⬆ Most cheese is made using a chemical created by GM.

If GM foods are clearly labelled, we can choose whether to buy them. In Europe, all products containing more than one per cent of GM food must have labels saying so. Other foods use GM science but not GM ingredients. Most cheese, for example, contains chemicals made by GM bacteria.

⬇ Look at the food labels in your larder.

At home, check the labels of foods in the fridge or larder to see if they contain GM ingredients.

In fact, not many food labels show you their GM ingredients. But many sweet items, including chocolate and ice cream, contain GM soya, as do cereals and some baby foods.

27

Do we need GM?

GM science is here to stay. But people disagree about how soon GM crops should be grown.

Other people do not think that GM foods should be sold in shops.

More people are buying foods that are grown using simple methods. They think that GM crops are not the best way to feed the world.

▷ **Tractors and other machines can help poor farmers.**

Supporters of GM say GM crops will one day help to feed the world. But many people feel there are other ways to solve world hunger.

For example, rich countries can help poorer ones by supplying equipment and training. Better management of farmland and water supplies can also provide more food.

△**These strawberries can grow without soil.**

Hydroponics is a method of growing crops without soil. The crops are supplied with water containing all the minerals they need to grow. This technique could be used to grow crops in places where there is plenty of water but the soil is poor. There would be less need to create GM crops that can grow in poor soil.

Organic farmers grow food using natural methods.

Organic farmers raise crops without using artificial weedkillers. They nourish their fields with manure and compost instead of chemical fertilisers. Instead of spraying their crops to control pests, they may encourage pest-eating insects, such as ladybirds.

Many people feel that foods grown using natural methods are better for you than GM crops.

Find out more! This scientist is growing GM peach and apple trees.

If you want to find out more about GM foods, try these useful websites:

- Monsanto (makes GM crops)
  www.monsanto.com
- Friends of the Earth
  www.foei.org
- Genewatch UK
  www.genewatch.org
- Biotechnology Australia
  www.biotechnology.gov.au
- Soil Association
  www. soilassociation.org
- The Food Standards Agency
  www.foodstandards.gov.uk
  www.foodstandards.gov.au

You decide!

Many people have strong views about GM foods. Some people feel GM crops are the way forward for farming.

Other people feel that the risks for both people and nature are too great.

Find out more about GM and discuss it with your friends. Then make up your own mind.

◁ 1. When are you eating GM Foods?

It is not always easy to know, but look out for GM foods at your local supermarket. The laws about GM labels changed in April 2004. All food that contains GM crops must now say so on the label.

Restaurants must also tell you when they use food that contains GM crops. For example, your chips may be fried in oil made from GM maize or soya beans.

2. Discuss GM with your class.

GM is often in the news these days. Ideas about GM vary from country to country. Listen out for news reports about GM. You can find out more using the internet and from books at your local library. Ask your teacher if you can discuss GM at school.

FOR	Against
• GM may help farmers grow more food.	• GM crops may affect wildlife.

Add your own points for and against.

3. Write a list of points for and against GM foods.

To make a list of points for and against GM foods, draw a line down a piece of paper. List the good things about GM on one side, and the drawbacks on the other side. Make up your own mind about GM.

GLOSSARY

Bacteria [singular: bacterium] – The tiny living things that are found everywhere.

Cells – The tiny units from which living things are made.

DNA – A molecule found inside cells, made up of four chemicals.

Evolve – When a particular type of plant or animal changes slowly over many generations, to suit its environment.

Gene – A section of DNA that carries instructions for a particular inherited feature, such as hair colour.

GM – Genetic Modification: the process of changing the genes of living things, so that they develop differently.

GM foods – Foods containing crops that have been altered using GM science.

Organic farming – A method of farming that does not use chemicals to kill weeds or pests.

Pesticide – A poison used to kill pests such as insects.

Species – A unique type of plant, animal, or other living thing.

INDEX

Photocredits

Abbreviations: l-left, r-right, b-bottom, t-top, c-centre, m-middle

Front cover c — Select Pictures. Front cover bl, 12ml, 15t, 18tl, 20br — Keith Weller/USDA. Front cover tl and br, 1, 3tr, 4l, 10ml, 13bm, 16tr, 16br, 17br, 18ml, 19tr, 21br, 29tr, 29bl — Scott Bauer/USDA. Front cover tr, back cover all, 4-5, 12tr, 14bm, 23tl, 25br, 26tr, 26mr, 27tl, 27ml, 27br — Stockbyte. 2mr, 18br, 21tl — Corel. 3mr, 7tr — Jack Dykinga/USDA. 3br, 30tr — Corbis. 6br, 15ml — Digital Stock. 7tl, 13bl, 17tr, 24mr, 28tr — Ken Hammond/USDA. 7bl, 27mr — Jim Pipe. 8bl — Brand X Pictures. 9tl, 19bl, 28c — Tim McCabe/USDA. 9tr, 11br — Photodisc. 11tl — Charles Herron/USDA. 11ml — Bill Tarpenning/USDA. 13tr — Russ Hanson/USDA. 15br, 20ml — USDA. 16mr — Sandra Silvers/USDA. 19c — John Deere. 22mr — US Fish & Wildlife Service. 23c — Corbis Royalty Free. 23br — Doug Buhler/USDA. 24tr, 24-25, 25bl — Peggy Greb/USDA. 26bl, 30bl — PBD.